Faith,
a Persistent Hunger

Joan Mitchell

Winston Press

Copyright © 1977 by Winston Press, Inc.
ISBN: 0-03-021261-8
Library of Congress Card Catalog Number: 77-72201

Printed in the United States of America

**Winston Press
430 Oak Grove
Minneapolis, MN 55403**

Photo Credits:
Rohn Engh 56
Rick Smolan 8, 38, 68, 84
Vivienne 4, 94

Biblical quotations in this book are from:

Common Bible, The Revised Standard Version
(RSV) Copyright© 1973 by Division of Christian
Education of the National Council of the Churches
of Christ in the United States of America.
Published by William Collins, Sons and Company, New York.

The New American Bible (NAB). Copyright© 1970
by Confraternity of Christian Doctrine, Washington, D.C.
Published by P.J. Kennedy & Sons, New York.

Contents

The Beginning

Prepare to imagine your own journey from birth to conception. Find a quiet corner in your home, away from everyone else, away from the TV, radio, telephone. Sit in a comfortable chair or on cushions on the floor. Close your eyes for a few minutes and try to empty your mind of things you've been thinking about or worrying about lately. Play a piece of classical instrumental music with long melodic phrases to help imagination. Read the poem on the next page to yourself — aloud, if you wish.

A sperm and an ovum join.
Cells begin to multiply.
I begin to take human shape.
I feel my arms forming, my fingers,
I feel my heart begin to beat.
My legs kick.
Slowly, my dark home grows smaller —
A force begins to push me down,
down into a narrow place.
I struggle for room to move.
I feel a force about to rocket me...
where?

Suddenly, I am surrounded by light!
I gasp. I breathe.
I am about to make my first sound
in the human world.

What do you want your first human sound to say? When you finish experiencing your imaginary birth, share your feelings with a friend.

This book is about believing, living, being born again and again. It is about feelings, confusion, experiences which restore your faith — and shake it. Some of the activities and questions will help you to explore yourself; some will help you explore the faith and feelings of others when you share them.

Because this book is both for reading and doing, you might want to find a friend to experience it with. Although faith is a deeply personal experience, it can gain strength when it is present in a group.

Chapter One

Believing, I Open and I Speak

Your first cry in the human world is followed by gurgles and burps, "dada" and "mine," then more and more words that express who you are. Among the words you use to speak of yourself are faith words. These express your dreams, your goals in life, your relationship with God. Today, many thousands of days after your first sound in the human world, what do you believe?

Which of the following statements of belief could you make right now?

— I believe the sun will come up tomorrow.
— I believe it is all right to step on cracks.
— I believe my house will be still there when I get home tonight.
— I believe the mechanic who fixes my brakes knows how to do it.
— I believe organized, citizen pressure groups are necessary to make corporations responsible for the environment.
— I believe my friends would stick up for me if I needed them.

— I believe my parents care about me.
— I believe I can make a difference in the future of the world.
— I believe something or someone very alive must have caused all living things to be.

Think about the following questions: What order do you see in the progression of these statements of belief? How is believing the sun will come up tomorrow different from believing in God? How many of the statements on the list do you believe? If you stopped believing part way down the list, what were your reasons for stopping? If you believed all the statements, why did you believe them?

Who Is God to You?

To be open to the possibility of God today is like going to a giant masquerade ball. The only person there is God, but God wears a thousand faces, one that expresses each person's relationship with him. Some of the identities are attractive and inviting, while others cause problems.

God the Has-Been: "Believe in God? Who's he? I believe in people, in big breakfasts and small cars, in returnable bottles and world peace."

To this person, only faith in humankind is alive. Faith in God is outmoded. God is out-of-date.

God the Scapegoat: "If God is so great and powerful, why are there wars and starvation? Why the terrible waste of the environment?"

To this person, God is responsible for death, hunger, and destruction. Seemingly infinite problems need an infinite cause. God has to take the blame.

God the Rock: "God used to be an answer. Now he's just another problem and no good to fall back on."

This person wants God to provide security. This person wants to say, in effect, "Since I accepted Jesus Christ as my Lord and Savior, he just does it all for me, like he puts the money in my pocket, the laces in my shoes." This person doesn't want to search and say, "I don't know who God is. I keep thinking today maybe I'll understand."

The statements below each describe God. Select the descriptions that express who God is to you. Add your own statements if you wish. Examine the statements you choose. What do they have in common? Who is your God? Explain to a friend who your God is, and ask your friend to react to your description. Does your idea of God cause problems? Does it make God fail, make him personal, make him irrelevant?

God is.... Check the statements you agree with. Add you own.

— The only being who loves me for myself.
— The computer that programmed the universe.
— A puppeteer who manipulates people like toys.
— An energy hinted at when a baby is born, when we fall in love.
— An unseen world soul that we are all a part of.
— A creator who believes everything he has made is very good.
— A force that became inert sometime between creation and today.
— A father who loves his children selflessly.
— Someone who forgives mistakes he lets me make.

— A being so beyond me that words fail to describe him.
— Someone who loves us enough to die for us.
— An eccentric being who created the world and forgot it.
— Someone who dares to let me be free.
— A being who gave me life.
— A lawgiver whose commands urge me to do right rather than wrong.
— The future, the end of all human striving.
— A being the human race will evolve into.
— A ruler whose power is freedom and love rather than force.
— A lover who urges me to come to the heavenly marriage feast.
— An idea created by past generations before human beings knew they could control nature and shape their world.
— The peace that will reign when all people live together in harmony.
— The perfect one who says I am sinful and makes me feel guilty.
— The one who cares that I become myself.

— A clown who created laughter when
   he made man free.

_____

_____

_____

Coming to faith and living in faith
involves a growth process. Jesus tells
Nicodemus in John's Gospel (3:3-8) that
coming to believe in him demands rebirth.
Birth is a dramatic moment. Nine months of
slow coming-to-be climax in the first breath
and first cry of a new being in a world
totally new to him or her. Believing is a
continuous challenge to be reborn.
   Faith, like birth, is a process, an ING, an
ongoing action. In both, there is a rhythm
like the rise and fall of the feet in walking or
the rise and fall of a melody in music. Birth
is coming-to-be, then being born. Faith is
seeking, then finding, then seeking again.
   The moment of physical birth only
begins the process of being born. In
children, birth continues dramatically.
Babies creep, crawl, and discover that their
legs take them places. A two-year-old plays
telephone with pliers, spoons, and keys but

fears the voice in a real phone. Then one day the youngster recognizes the voice in the phone and wants to answer every call.

Over and over in the process of believing, we open ourselves to further growth, to new births. Over and over, we hunger to savor life more fully. Over and over, the believer seeks the presence of God. Faith is like a relentless hunger, an insatiable appetite for the wide, high, deep meaning of life and the divine.

Understanding the following lines from a Walt Whitman poem, "Song of Myself," may clarify the processes of growth and rebirth:

A child said What is the grass? fetching it to me with full hands,
How could I answer the child? I do not know what it is any more than he.

The poem suggests that the familiar, tangled brown and green tufts we see day after day are mysterious and unknown. Grass, like everything else, does not fully explain itself. Such simple questions often quicken our appetite for deeper understanding.

In the poem the question "What is the grass?" begins the coming-to-be of a new understanding of grass. In the rhythm of the poem a birth follows the coming-to-be. After the question, Whitman writes a series of new descriptions of grass: a flag woven of hopeful green stuff, the handkerchief of the Lord, a child, the uncut hair of graves. Faith, too, is a continuous birth. It has the rhythm of growth — of planting, then reaping; of seeking, then finding; of opening more fully to life, then discovering more fully its meaning.

Go outside and sit in the grass, and ask yourself: What is the grass?

This book is about each of us believing. The subject is the personal faith that originates in the question, " What do I make of the fact that I am? " Creedal faith is held in common by many people.

Personal faith is often identified with creedal faith; that is, with allegiance to the system of beliefs of a church or religion. The creeds of churches and the doctrines of religions develop slowly. They are carefully worded statements debated and hammered out, often by thousands of people, over several centuries. As they come to us, creeds may hide the process that gave them birth.

"Jesus is God and man" is a statement demanding acceptance rather than offering an invitation into the process of discovering who Jesus is. "I believe in God, the Father almighty, Creator of heaven and earth," states rather than invites. Creeds are meant to be stated by believers. The word "creed" comes from the Latin word for "I believe." It leaves no room for questions or doubts.

How does a person come to believe in a Creator? Can people who take for granted the fact that they are alive state truly that they believe someone created them?

How does faith come to be? What gives faith birth and rebirth? What opens us to the possibility of God? What gives us a feeling of the presence of God? The grass? A friend? The self? Anything that is?

My believing may not end
in accepting a creed.
But when I live in the world with its people,
beneath the sky and between the horizons,
grappling with the fact that I am
but have not created myself,
I enter into the process of believing,
of answering for myself.
Me believing is me growing
as a person who answers for myself.

Think of five things that you believe personally. Write them down. Keep them in a notebook if you wish, add to them, refer to them throughout your use of this book.

Self. Nature. Other people. God, the mysterious ground of living things. How are these bound together? How do we feel, live, and interpret the connections among all these things? Christians believe the Scriptures record how God has revealed himself, how God makes himself known and invites us to friendship with him and with each other. But revelation is also something each of us experiences as we interpret our own lives.

The Biblical stories of God revealing himself and inviting people to a relationship of faith and friendship are in a real sense our stories. As we live and interpret our experience, we find ourselves living the story of Job, of Sarah, of Jonah, of Peter, of Paul. Our biblical tradition tells us God wants to be found. We need to live and search in order to experience the living, the searching, the finding our tradition treasures.

Coming to believe in God depends on staying in touch with the fact that I live and move and have being. It is through my own personal existence that I feel, live, and interpret the mysterious ground out of which I and all living things come. It is the me of each of us who watches icicles drip, who remembers Mother's Day, who questions the origin of life and the purpose of living. We each participate in revelation through our personal faith. In revelation, something unknown becomes known. We have all struggled with an impossible problem until a light switches on and we see the solution clearly. In the history of religions, the word *revelation* is reserved for describing divine manifestations in the world of human beings.

In his study of religious experience, *The Sacred and the Profane,* Mircea Eliade calls such a manifestation a *hierophany.* A hierophany is a breakthrough of the divine into the human world. A stone, a mountain, another person, a burning bush, or an altar becomes alive with the awesome, powerful presence of someone or something totally *other* than human.

The burning bush which Moses saw remained a bush, yet at the same time appeared engulfed in a consuming fire. When the divine reveals itself and shows itself forth in a natural object, this is a hierophany.

The word *revelation* makes us think of burning bushes, of extraordinary and clear manifestations of God, of breakthroughs that knock over all ten pins of a person. Perhaps revelation sometimes feels like that: Moses at the burning bush; Isaiah before the temple altar; Peter, James, and John at the Transfiguration; the centurion at the cross; Paul on the road to Damascus.

But revelation is also something we seek in feeling, living, and interpreting our lives.

I will understand God no better
than I understand myself.
My own experience of living is
the only raw material I have
for coming to faith.
My experience may include
reading the Bible,
growing up in a doctrinal tradition, and
understanding the beliefs of others.

But it is me living who
becomes me believing.

In the Beginning we do not know what happened.
In My Beginning a sperm and an ovum joined,
long before I remember.

In the Beginning of my knowing and
remembering life,
I discovered that I AM.

I am my life, body, mind, eyes, heart, talents,
fingers, feet, imagination, skin, backbone, will.

Like billions of other people,
like toads and grass,
like galaxies of stars,
and universes of galaxies, I AM.
And so again,
What do I make of the fact that I am?

We are all closed until we speak ourselves.
A human being can open,
                    speak,
                         reveal self,
                              others,
                                   flowers.

　　My belief in the ability of a mechanic,
the love of a friend, the reality of God, is
tied to my self-understanding.
　　It is difficult to describe the process of
revelation. The experience of God, a person,
or even a single blade of grass is a
wordless happening. It is never totally
expressible. Yet, to know and understand

what happens in our lives, we must express ourselves. What we communicate reveals the meaning of what we experience. What we have no words for remains concealed, so we open up again to living, seeking further meaning.

The process of believing begins in opening, in a willingness to experience all that grass or anything is. Over and over the believer opens himself or herself

to the wide,
to the deep,
to the high of living,
to the mysterious origin
and purpose of it all.

Our experience builds up. We must express it in order to discover its meaning. We are amazed by the eerie streaks of the Northern Lights, by the depth of a friend's insights, by the concern of someone we hardly know. Then we express and interpret our living, and a belief, an idea, an insight is born. As we speak our living, we discover its meaning. We experience revelation in interpreting life.

To explore how differently we each express ourselves, take a walk with a friend and try mimicking each other's walks.

In your notebook, list ten actions that express yourself. Analyze them. What do they reveal about you? What do they reveal about what you believe?

If you can, draw your idea of God. Have a four-or five-year-old draw his or her idea of God. Compare your picture and the child's. How does the me of each artist affect his or her drawing?

The Inexpressible Silence

"Explain yourself." These words could be making fun or they could be accusing. They could also be unanswerable. "What are you doing here?" At its deepest level this simple, everyday question touches the inexplainable fact that *I am*. How do I explain that I am? What do I make of it? The answer is often silence. What is this silence, and what does it mean?

I am myself within constant hearing of the silence. Rowing at sunrise on a misty lake, two friends absorb the beauty in silence. Another night, a wide, bright circle rays outward around the moon. A bare plum tree stands silhouetted against the night sky. A wind moves through the banana leaves, clinks the wind chimes. The silent wind seems to speak.

The news reports a couple missing in the mountains on a ski trip. The woman is a friend. What are the words for the feeling that someone you knew alive may be dead? Silence drowns all words.

I realize someone trusts me.
There is no word for why.
I wonder why I was born.
I am a question to myself.
I hear the silence.

In the silence, many people hear hints of God. Those who feel God's presence usually find no adequate words to express what happens. God seems so awesome and *other* than us that his presence cannot be described fully. Yet, it is in their ordinary lives that people experience God.

How do we talk about God? How do we say what we hear in the silence? Since we feel, live, and interpret the mysterious ground of all living things so uniquely and so inexpressibly, perhaps the best name for God is THE UNNAMEABLE.

My deepest experiences of myself, of others, of nature, of the unnameable are wordless, unspeakable. These are the moments of opening and seeking. Moments of stammered words follow — me expressing, revealing the meaning of the experience.

The silence of the unnameable
becomes language to many who listen to it.

Give yourself some time alone or with a
friend in silence. Try to get in touch with the
fact that you are, then share your feelings.
Find some way to express how you feel
about being alive.

Stammering
the Inexpressible

Faith in other people, in life, in oneself,
in a name for the unnameable, involves a
creative tension between the expressible
and the inexpressible.

In his book, *Moses*, the Jewish
philosopher Martin Buber says, "It is laid
upon the stammering to bring the voice of
Heaven to Earth."

Stammering characterizes the speech
of someone trying to communicate a deep
experience. No matter what our ability with
words, the awakening to the fact that I am,
the amazement I feel watching a spring
runlet tumble over a tree root, waking the
silence of the winter woods into sound, the
birth of a baby, the death of a friend — none
of these things are totally communicable.

We seek words to help us unveil and savor an experience. But words also limit our experience, limit our ability to make present to ourselves all that we are window to. Like all words, words of faith conceal and reveal. The unnameable will be named in stammering.

We often live at an "I'm fine, how are you?" level. We have to. We are not always in touch with the amazement of living.

When an experience is fresh, the word that reveals its meaning is a speaking word. A speaking word is alive with the experience it expresses. It stammers some of the incommunicable silence. It stammers me feeling, living, interpreting, believing.

A spoken word is a word many people know and use. It is a too familiar word. Time and overuse have dulled its power to communicate.

For example, the "beat" talk of the fifties popularized "cool," "square," and "like." Like, it was *in,* like, to start every sentence with "like." In the sixties "cool" cooled as a popular expression. "With it," "neat" and "groovy" each had their turn. In the early seventies "cool" again warmed up to a speaking word.

Groups sometimes create their speaking slang word. In religious circles, words like "commitment," "community," and "renewal" have had their day as speaking words and have dulled to spoken words from overuse.

A speaking word "really says it." We feel what it communicates. A spoken word is a limp, dull word. It is like a fact that fits in the head but neither affects nor speaks to our lives.

Think of examples from current slang of speaking words. Think of examples of spoken words. Does your occupation or religion have speaking words and spoken words?

Sit on your hands and say what you mean. Hands, grins, and frowns fill in for most of us when our words stammer. With a friend try telling the funniest thing that happened to you in the last week. Sit on your hands and say what you mean. In fact, sit with your back to the other person. Rely solely on your own words to communicate with the other person.

Repeat what you each hear the other say. How well do you succeed in communicating your experience? Try to determine when your words seem to be speaking words, when they seem to be spoken words.

Spoken words for the unnameable can sometimes become speaking words for us if we recreate the experience that gave them birth. Exodus 15 is a song of thanksgiving for Israel's escape from the Egyptians through the Red Sea. It is one of the most ancient pieces of oral tradition in the Hebrew Bible. We read it today:

I will sing to the Lord
for he has triumphed gloriously,
horse and rider
he has thrown into the sea.
The Lord is my strength and my song,
and he has become my salvation....
(Exodus 15:1-2 RSV)

We read *triumphed*, *salvation* and *strength*, and think, "the usual God words." They say nothing about me, living. But change *salvation* to *liberation*, and we have a speaking word for our time.

Write a song of thanksgiving for a freeing experience you have had. Or sing or play a contemporary song that expresses what it's like to be freed. Compare the feeling you get reading Exodus 15 with the feeling you express in your own song or find in a contemporary song.

Sometimes, spoken words for the unnameable become speaking words because of a personal experience. This is Harry Yacher's story:

Harry Yacher could care less. He didn't let things get to him. I met him my first day at Amalgamated when I was getting chewed out about putting some stuff in the wrong warehouse. Harry came up to me, "Hey man," he said, "don't take it so hard. It was your first mistake. Besides, the super is always mean on Mondays."

Harry and I had lunch together that day — and every work day since. We got to be good friends. Harry is a free spirit. He doesn't let work or anything else get him down.

That is, he didn't until the accident. I heard that two of the kids in Harry's neighborhood had been run over and killed. They'd been jumping car bumpers and sliding on their heels down the icy streets. What I didn't know was that Harry's younger brother had been with the kids. I saw Harry at work, but we didn't talk until after the funerals.

It was a Saturday morning. Kids were playing outside as we walked up Fiftieth Street on our way to the gym. One little boy was pulling his sister as fast as he could down the sidewalk in a saucer. He nearly rammed into us. He seemed to love running so much it didn't matter where he was going.

Harry was quiet. He stared at the kids playing until we passed them. It wasn't like Harry to just walk. The snow was snowball perfect, but he didn't seem to notice. We came to a corner. I walked halfway across the street before I realized that Harry had stopped. I turned around. When he saw me looking, he started across the street. I finally had to say something.

"For God's sake, Harry, what's wrong with you?" Harry kept walking, staring at his feet, like his feet were the only things in the whole world. We reached another corner. Harry looked up and down the street, then crossed alongside me. "Harry, I'm going home. You're not into going to the gym this morning anyway."

"Wait up," he muttered.

"OK, but you're acting so strange. What in hell is wrong?"

"I don't know. I've never felt like this before."

"Try to explain it. I feel like I'm walking with a ghost."

We walked farther. I could tell Harry was trying to begin.

"Is it because of those kids that got run over?" I finally asked him.

"I guess so," he said.

"But it's happened before. You said you broke your arm doing the same thing."

"I know."

"You barely knew the kids." I was getting desperate. "Harry, I can't stand it. Either tell me or I'm going home."

"I knew the kids." I could tell he was ready so I didn't say anything. "I knew them. My brother was with them. My brother could be dead like those kids. I was out wrestling with them in the snow after supper, then I went up to the drugstore and it happened. I wanted to shout to somebody, 'They were just playing. For God's sake, it was only fun.' But who do I scream at? That's how I felt at first. Mad. It wasn't fair. I just couldn't fit it together. It's like I always thought God was good, you know. This unfair thing, this crazy chance, it just couldn't happen."

I was the one not saying anything now. I understood what Harry was saying, but there wasn't anything to say back. He was right. We walked along again in quiet.

"Then there was the funeral. I walked up to the church from home, not thinking much of anything. I was tired from being mad. I got across the street from the church, and my feet just stopped. I couldn't go across. I was sweating and scared. I've never felt like that before. I knew I was risking my life to step into that street. I wanted to stay alive. It scared me to be alive because something could kill me. It was like the most precious thing in the world to be alive. Then suddenly my feet just started going again, and I found myself in church. I was sitting there. I recognized my jacket. I thought this must be me, but I felt like this stranger. I remember lots of people in the church and the singing, but that's all, except for something the minister read. It went something like, 'God is close to the broken-hearted.' That line stuck in my mind like nothing ever does. I remember thinking, 'That's dumb.' But it stayed in my mind as if it was the only thing there. Then the words changed, and I heard 'open-hearted.' It was like watching all this happen to somebody else right inside my skin. Then I had this feeling of quiet. I felt sort of satisfied. Those words *broken* and *open* were there, just there in my mind. Then I realized what I knew. I felt my pulse in my head. I knew my heart was going to stop — the next beat. But it didn't. I was alive. And that was what I knew. I didn't understand why or anything. I've had this scared kind of broken feeling ever since, but it's a good feeling, too."

We walked on. I remember every street we crossed.

The old song of the Psalm, "Yahweh is near to the broken-hearted," became a new song when it became Harry's song. Old words of faith became the speaking words for his experience.

What experiences in your life have deeply affected your words for the unnameable?

Paul Tillich, a Lutheran theologian, claimed that God is who we mean when all words fail. If God could be totally translated into words, we would possess him. Yet, in our experience we find we cannot possess even another person. We experience ourselves and others as both known and unknown, as revelation and secret.

When we call someone "out of it" or "just a clown," we box him or her in. We limit a personality to a first impression or a strange outfit. Words for God box him in and can box us out of any need to experience the unnameable for ourselves.

If we see faith as allegiance to others' names for the unnameable, faith becomes a matter of learning "God language" much as one learns French. The spoken words of others may or may not become speaking words for us. The spoken words of others may shield us from speaking our own experience.

Doctrines, laws, others' names for God, and others' beliefs cannot take away from us the necessity of responding personally to the fact that we exist. Ministers and priests explain and preserve the Word of God, the whole collection of faith-words from our ancestors in faith. They should be not only guardians of the Word, but also guardians of the silence, of the incommunicability of any experience — especially the experience of the unnameable.

Psalm 103 is a song describing God as kind and forgiving. Read it. Put yourself in the place of the person who wrote it. What must have been that person's experience of God? Write your own psalm describing your experiences of God. Take examples of what God is like from your own life.

Each of us has a lifetime
to respond in stammering
to the beat of life in our veins.
I am not a self I have no words for.
I grow in understanding of myself
as I express myself.
I will name the unnameable
no better than I speak myself,
for only through myself do I experience all
of life and give it meaning.

Every person is a maker of meaning.
A bud in spring calls for a response,
for a word that gives meaning
to the melting of the frozen world.
Faith does not exist
if my faith is not me, believing,
if it is not me, fighting to name
the silence between two selves,
if it is not me, trying to express the silence
between myself and endless sea and sky,
if it is not me,
shouting my word to the silence
out of which I come and into which I go.

Think of today as a birth day.
Something of ourselves is born each day. At
the beginning of the chapter, you thought
about what your first cry in the world spoke.
What is the word for your birth today?

Share your words with a friend. In sharing them, you will be making a revelation together.

CONFUSIONS, FEELINGS, BROKEN IDEALS fragment me believing. Faith would be easier to find or to dodge if it were only a set of doctrines to accept or reject. But my faith is me believing, me opening to life, my expressing my living into the community of human beings, into the unnameable silence.

The next three chapters explore the confusions, feelings, and disillusionments that keep you from finding personal faith.

Chapter Two

Confusion

Confusion is like having a head full of feathers. The feathers are ideas. They have sharp ends that poke and jab and fluffy ends that tickle. Open your hand to pick one up and two more fly loose.

Understanding the difference between faith and THE faith, personal and imaginary, God now and God then, may put some order in the confusion.

The Headache Questionnaire
(The believer's guide to more comfortable confusion.)

Directions: Following are statements by different people about the headaches of finding faith. Put a check in the space beside each statement that expresses your own confusion. When you finish, use the answer analyzer following the statements. The analyzer will tell you which of the sections in the chapter to use next to become more comfortably confused.

_____ 1. "Everybody believes something different about God, so what am I supposed to believe?"

_____ 2. "I wish Jesus were here today. Then I could make up my own mind about him."

_____ 3. "Every church says it's the right one, so which one is the true religion?"

_____ 4. "You just have to think of Jesus in your mind. Nobody knows what he was like, so he's whoever you make him."

_____ 5. "The only people I know who go to church are older people who think they're going to go to heaven that way."

_____ 6. "Every minister has his or her own version of what everybody else ought to do. Why don't ministers agree?"

_____ 7. "I don't condemn the Bible because I've never read it. I probably won't read it either. I'd rather read something modern."

_____ 8. "I believe in God but not the way the churches say."

_____ 9. "I'm afraid God can't be modernized."

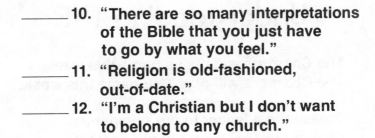

_____ 10. "There are so many interpretations of the Bible that you just have to go by what you feel."

_____ 11. "Religion is old-fashioned, out-of-date."

_____ 12. "I'm a Christian but I don't want to belong to any church."

Answer Analyzer. The section of this chapter called "Understanding The" answers questions raised in 1, 3, 6, 8, and 12. See pages 42 to 49.

"A Personal Problem" explores the questions raised in 2, 4, and 10. See pages 50 to 53.

"Faith Then and Now" discusses questions raised in 5, 7, 9, and 11. See pages 53 to 55.

Understanding THE

The Chargers will play a game this week.
The Chargers will play THE game this week.

Gleason is a leader in our company.
Gleason is THE leader in our company.

In twenty seconds or less, explain the difference *the* makes in the second of each pair of statements.

When THE is used to single out a one and only, THE becomes a closing word. The game of the week. THE faith. THE cuts off one game from every other. It singles out a set of beliefs as one, only, complete, and beyond conversation with other beliefs, personal or creedal.

The early Christians believed that Jesus was Lord, that he was God as well as human. The meaning the early Christians found in Jesus has been passed on, but not the process of discovering the meaning. Successive generations have heard the collections of words for what the experience of Jesus meant to the first Christians. Their *wordless* experience of the unnameable in Jesus is not always passed on.

The life and message of Jesus becomes so many second, third, and fourth hand accounts — boring and irrelevant compared to our own living experiences. Faith becomes THE faith, a one-and-only set of beliefs, divorced from the experience it once expressed.

Traditions must pass on the challenge to future generations to enter into the process of making meaning. To believe in Jesus is to believe in a doing man, a process man. To accept the Christian tradition is not to consent to so many words, but to dare to live in the human scene as Jesus lived.

The number of interpretations of Scripture, the plurality of Christian denominations and world religions, the variety of people in our lives who have definite beliefs, all are perplexing. If our faith is THE faith, sharing faith becomes a stock market of competing opinions. Sharing personal faith is not trading and evaluating beliefs. Personal faith is confessed, declared. It is me expressing my life, my relationship with God and other people. When we speak our own faith words, we may also find them in conversation with the words of friends, relatives, or the words of Job, Sarah, or Paul.

It is as if the unnameable were a great tree. Each of us sees the tree from a different angle. To share faith is to move around the tree, seeing what others have seen.

Interview five people of different ages with beliefs different from your own. Ask each person these questions:
— Who are the three most important people in your life? Why?
— What was the most influential experience of God you have had? What was it like?
— Is there any difference between your own personal faith and the doctrines of the church you belong to? If so, what?
— If you believe in God, why do you believe in God?
— What is the best name for God as you have experienced him in your life?

When the interviews are complete, talk about your findings with a friend. Perhaps you will want to analyze your findings in order to determine if the different age groups or religious groups responded to the question in similar ways.

Centers create THEs. Human beings live from centers. Like traditions, centers can become "one and only."

Medieval maps often pictured Jerusalem as the center of the world because it was the holy city of Christendom. Scholars have found examples of primitive tribes that lay down and died when an enemy destroyed their totem, the center of their world.

World is a word for an organized environment. For an environment to be a world, a home for human beings, it must be founded and organized around centers. Today, our centers are no longer sacred poles or holy mountains. Friends, family, work or school may be our centers.

Although the present pace of change threatens the core each of us lives from, it also makes our need for centers more clear. In his book, *Future Shock*, Alvin Toffler predicts a breakdown of the will to live if centers are destroyed. He gives examples: the stimuli of battle has so overloaded the "adaptive powers" of some soldiers that they become indifferent to living; a soldier with little sleep after weeks in the field, bombarded by bullets and mortar, finally just lies laughing on his back waiting to die. Toffler cites studies of stress that indicate that a widow or widower has a 40 percent higher chance of serious illness or death in the first six months after the loss of a spouse. A life too fragmented or too overloaded with change is unliveable.

Visiting or moving to a new city is an experience of the fragmented life. Every house looks the same. The tallest building is always visible but seems to change places from day to day. None of the vacant lots hold memories, nor does the city park hide secret thinking places. No friends make one house stand out from the others. Not until you live in the city and find friends and a hillside for thinking, will the fragmented metropolis become a world for you.

To demonstrate this tendency to live from centers in yourself, draw a map of your town, city, or township. Compare and contrast your map with one drawn up by a friend. What differences do you find? Does either map look like a road map picked up at a gas station, or can you tell from the maps where each person's center lies?

Each person's centers will be THE centers to him or her. The lives of each of us must revolve around key people and places if our lives are to be liveable.

Centers become THEs (the one right center) only when we forget how important the process of organizing the environment is to *each* person and, instead, defend our own centers as the only *ones*. We forget process and stand on content. We shut ourselves off from the centers of others and hole up in our own.

Think or your attitudes toward your church or your job. Are either of them THE center to you?

A closing word about THE: Confusion between faith and THE faith often hinders people from stammering their own faith words. If a person accepts a church creed without experiencing the unnameable for himself or herself, that person becomes a believer in other people's words. A person who never learns any of the traditional faith words begins at the beginning without any benefit of the experience of hundreds of generations. Coming to faith is a process involving both learning THE faiths of others and expressing one's own experience.

The traditions we make or accept, the centers we find, are uniquely our own. Perhaps the vitality of nature — moss sending up spore stems before the snow is gone — symbolizes a person's desire to live. Perhaps I come to my understanding of the Commandment, "Thou shall not kill," when I blast a pheasant out of a fall sky. I feel a strange chilling guilt when I pick up the richly-colored body by its limp and bloody neck.

Personal faith may be awakened by a parent paying attention, or by a friend who notices I am depressed and wants to help. What stirs us to believing will be an individual experience.

THE is a closing word when it singles out a belief as a one and only, as a fact and not a mystery to live out. A church may say THE, or a person may say THE. When we say THE, we establish a belief as final. Those who believe it are in, those who don't are out. Faith becomes a content to be accepted. Faith is no longer a process of opening to life and expressing its meaning, of discovering the traditions and centers of others and wording them for myself.

Conversation is one way out of the confusion of varying faith words. In conversation, believing becomes sharing rather than competing.

Write three statements expressing your most important personal beliefs. The beliefs do not have to involve God. Exchange statements with a friend. If you do not understand each other's words, discuss the statements until your beliefs are clear.

For each statement, write down THE church doctrine you know that comes closest to expressing the same belief. Discuss the results. Are there church doctrines for all of your beliefs? Are you in conflict with church doctrines? With others' beliefs?

A "Personal" Problem

"I wish Jesus were here today. Then I could make up my own mind about him."

"Nobody has seen God. God is whatever or whoever you make him. God is personal to each person."

"You just have to think of Jesus in your mind. Nobody knows what he was like, so he's whoever you imagine he is."

"You just have to go by what you feel about God."

Confusion and headache fill these statements. What similar confused feelings have you experienced? Think about how you feel toward your parents or friends.

What color best expresses God? What does God look like? What does God sound like? Talk about these questions with a friend. Explain the reasons for your responses to the questions. Where did your information come from?

Gather examples of Japanese, African, and Indian artistic expressions of God or Jesus. Where do you think these artists got their ideas of what God or Jesus was like?

Ask a friend the following questions about yourself. Write down his or her answers, and then give your answers.

Switch roles and try to answer your friend's questions about himself or herself.

What is my name? _____

What color is my hair? _____

What is my favorite song? _____

What is my favorite sport? _____

What is my favorite color? _____

What person do I most admire? _____

What do I care most about?

What is my most valuable talent?

What is the most important thing I
will achieve in my life?

What do I believe about God?

How many questions could each of you
answer correctly about the other? Which
questions could you answer from
observation; which from knowing each
other? Which questions could neither of
you answer?

Does another person's personality
depend on how we feel about him or her?
Can we make up or imagine what another
person is like? Can we imagine what God is
like? What do you mean when you say,
"God is personal to me."?
Personal feelings and imagination can
create the self and the God each of us
believes in. Personal feelings can trap us in
ourselves. Yet it is also through our own

feelings, imagination, and experiences that we understand each other and come closer to naming the unnameable.

What we believe about each other or the unnameable or ourselves does not come only from inside us, nor does it come only from outside us. Faith is born in the meeting of our insides with the world outside. If we each lived in a totally made-up world of feelings and imaginings, we would live in dream worlds. Yet the world and its people are not the same to each of us.

I sit in my house and you sit in your house; between us is silence. I really exist and you really exist, but we do not exist for each other. Similarly, it is possible for us to exist within the unnameable silence without realizing it. The unnameable may be within us or beyond us without our knowing.

Faith keeps us open to more than we can see at any one time. Faith is a learned expectation of surprise. I open myself to life and express the purpose of my living.

Faith Then...

Find pictures of nature, a stained glass window, a cherub or Michelangelo's

God the Father, church buildings, people communicating or helping, earth in space, a cross. Choose the picture that comes closest to expressing what you believed about God as a child. Explain your choice to a friend. Listen to the reasons your friend chose the picture he or she chose.

Each choose the picture that comes closest to expressing what each of you believes now, and explain these choices. Are the then and now pictures you chose the same? Are the two your friend chose the same? If not, discuss what has made your faith change. Has it changed for the better or for the worse? In what ways?

... and Now

Faith grows as the person grows. My understanding of God will not go beyond my understanding of myself. It is through myself that I experience life, others, and the unnameable. Only I can speak myself in faith.

Many people see the human race growing in the same ways individuals mature. Many see God as being no longer necessary for sophisticated modern people.

Others reject the idea of God as judge. Many continue to believe in a provident God who has all of human history planned. Many now find God within rather than above us. The question we all face is: can God be modernized?

At the end of *Kaddish*, a symphony finished by Leonard Bernstein on the day the late President John F. Kennedy was shot, the lead singer describes God as a partner to human beings in creation. Humanity has grown up. Now God must believe in people just as people have traditionally believed in God. Together they create or destroy the earth.

Perhaps, like Bernstein, we must dare to express our living for all to hear. We must dare to go beyond the known names and ideas of the unnameable.

If you can borrow *Kaddish* from a local library, listen to it with a friend and discuss it. You may need copies of the text in front of you.

Listen to Bernstein's *Mass*, to *Jesus Christ Superstar*, or to *Godspell*. Who is God to the composers of each of these works? What are the experiences they express in their music?

Chapter Three

Feelings

**Feelings,
gnaw,
bite,
wrench,
explode within
our unfolding selves.**

Among young adults, the struggles that most often generate strong, upsetting feelings include the need for independence, the need for acceptance, and the need for self-worth.

Faith problems can be feeling problems in disguise.

Read over the following snatches of conversation about faith problems. Then write an imaginary conversation between yourself and a friend. Use the excerpts to create the conversation. Add to them. Adapt them. Try to say what you believe or don't believe, and how you feel about what you think you should believe.

- Everybody's getting mad
- Missing the whole point
- God gives you strength
- God isn't that pastor
- Too idealized
- Find your own interpretation
- Religion is a bunch of
- Church is OK if
- Religion is personal to me
- I do my own worrying
- I can get the same feeling
- If you only look at your own point of view
- I believe what I believe
- What turns me off is
- When I go to church
- Mine is loving people
- Celebrate is what I mean
- I use church to organize my week
- I wonder what my mom is thinking
- If they'd get off my back

— You can't condemn it
— I work my own problems out
— I'm always questioning
— Putting other people first
— A peace reached within yourself, a love
— I think it's stupid to talk to God
— If you want to believe you're going to
— I don't believe like that
— Someone to turn to in a jam
— I want God to run my life
— Think of God as a friend
— So my life is changed
— God is
— Jesus Christ is
— If it's going to happen, it's going to happen

Have a friend write an imaginary conversation. When your conversations are written, read each other's. After reading your friend's conversation, tell him or her where his or her strong feelings about faith seem to lie. Switch roles. Do you each have aggravated, negative feelings? Positive, urgent feelings? Settled, matter-of-fact feelings?

This chapter explores three common tensions: finding *independence*, finding *acceptance*, and finding *self-worth*. Do any of the feelings that come out in your friend's conversation reflect tensions in these areas?

Are any of your problem feelings caused *only* by faith matters? Which of your feelings seem caused by both growing and faith problems? For example, you resent never being given responsibility at work, and you mind it when your parents or friends pressure you into going to church. Do your resentments flow from a need for greater independence? Do you specifically find going to church a problem?

Identifying your feelings and their causes may help you discover what you believe and who the me believing really is.

Independence

"Don't tell me what to do."

Why not? Can't the advice of another person be valuable? Does each person have to make every mistake for him or herself? What do you mean when YOU say "Don't tell me what to do!" What are you most touchy about being told to do?

"These Jesus people will stop you on the street and try to convert you on the spot."

What experiences of someone trying to convert you to his or her beliefs have you had? How did the experiences make you feel? What makes a difference in whether or not you will listen?

Imagine or role play a conversation about faith between a young man and his mother. The conversation raises a question many parents have: "How do I give my children faith?" Can faith be given by one person to another? If so, how?

What kind of statement by your parents makes you want to reject their beliefs? Try to pinpoint what makes you feel you have to be free of their influence.

"Rejecting the beliefs of my parents is necessary to discover what I want to stand for myself." Do you agree? Why or why not?

Who do you know who seems to be independent? What freedoms do you associate with independence? Having a car? Having a good job? Living alone?

What decisions have you made on your own? Did they work out? How did you feel about making a decision on your own?

Have you fought for something you believed? What was it? How did it feel? Did you feel confident that you were right? Did you look for support for your belief?

What do you think is a good symbol of independence?

Acceptance

"When somebody else shows you you're somebody, it really helps. Concern for you makes you feel wanted. You need people who can see you as a total — good and bad."

How many people do you feel you have to wear masks for to show mostly your good points or your bad points? Do you feel that wearing masks is sometimes necessary? When? Why or why not?

Have a friend tell you four of his or her best qualities and four of his or her worst qualities. Do you agree with what he or she says? Tell your friend what you consider your four best and worst qualities. Does he or she agree with your assessment of yourself? Do you feel you wear masks around each other?

"This may sound funny, but I really believe in God."

"Well, I'm probably in the minority, but I don't believe there's a God. That's why I wanted to talk about it, because I figured I'd better get something talked into me."

How can two people be hesitant about stating exactly opposite points of veiw? Is it what the two speakers are going to say that makes them feel uncomfortable? Or would these same feelings occur about whatever they said? Why?

Keep a list of the number of times a day you say "This may sound funny, but..." or "I don't want to say this because it's so weird," or "Everybody's going to laugh." Such statements show fear of disapproval. What I believe gets mixed up and tossed about with my need to feel I belong and am respected by a group. In what situations do your "This is dumb, but..." feelings come out?

A faith problem may be a feeling problem in disguise.

Self~Worth

"Self-worth is part of faith. If you constantly feel a sense of failure and nonrecognition, you don't know where you are." What do you think about this statement?

Exchange "I am" statements with a friend. Each write I AM at the top of a sheet of paper. Then write twenty "I am...." statements abut yourself. (For example: I am impatient. I am generous.) When you have finished, exchange and read each other's statements. React to them. Describe your friend in terms of what he or she wrote. Have your friend do the same for you. You may want to use symbolic descriptions. Describe your friend as an animal, a color, an inanimate object. You may want to respond to the other person's description of you.
What did you learn about yourself?

Think about these questions privately: Do other people see more in you than you do yourself? What qualities do others recognize in you that you do not see in

yourself? Does anyone see what you think
is best in yourself? Why or why not?

Daydreaming, Sunday 11AM

You live believing every day yet
Sundays come around fast and long
sometimes. Some people are always there. I
wonder if believing is easier for them than
for me. They seem so sure.
I feel there's a journey inside me that no
maps chart. "1,395 minutes from Reno to
where?" I remember the sign from this
summer. I live a question that walks
wherever I go. The question is me. Do I go
barefoot to feel the dirt beneath my feet or
kneel before everything taller than I am? Do
I tell my questions to the wind, follow a star,
thumb a ride? Jesus might pick me up . Or,
is trying all the time to be a reason for
myself enough?
My life is round like the earth. I walk to
the horizon in my mind, to the place where
what I know meets the dark future and
beyond. Sometimes I feel like a motorboat
penetrating a dark sea. I think I understand
myself. Then I watch the wake of my
motorboat smooth over into impenetrable
black glass. For me faith is living in a light

that touches darkness, in words that touch silence.

Jesus talked in strange symbols, like when he said, "I am the light of the world. No follower of mine shall ever walk in darkness; no, he shall possess the light of life." (John 8:12) That was the reading today. The "light of life" line stuck in my mind. I suppose it means we'll have the light of Jesus' way of doing things, or we'll have God's life. But I never understand what that is.

What if Jesus meant his followers will have the light of their own lives? What if he was trying to say why he became a man, trying to say that the life of a man will be a light to him? It's like each of us has the light of his or her own existence. We have the beat of life in our own veins to live from. Suppose Jesus was trying to get us to take ourselves seriously?

Perhaps he's saying, "search for the secret of yourself." Perhaps he showed us just how far one man's life could go toward being all he could dream to be. My life is the only thing I have that no one else has. The light of life. Am I the secert I look for?

Chapter Four

The Faithbreakers

**To break is to violate,
to burst like a bubble.**

**But has an ideal or an idol
been smashed?**

**Faithbreakers cause shock, doubt,
disillusionment, person-quakes, tremors,
upheavals of my me.**

**Which of the situations listed below
come close to expressing personquakes
you have had?**
   **— I left money on my desk and had it
   stolen.**
   **— I find out my best friend has a date
   with a man she insisted I should
   never go out with.**
   **— A driver across the intersection
   signals a left turn, so I make a left
   turn in front of him. He doesn't mean
   to turn and hits my right rear fender.**
   **— My parents say I can go to a college I
   really want to go to eight hundred**

miles from home. I get accepted, and they say I can't go. I find out they said yes because they were sure I wouldn't get in.

— I have a mechanic fix the clutch linkage on my car. On the way home all the gears go out but low.

— I call a woman I've dated several times and ask her to a New Year's Eve party. She says she doesn't know if she can go. Two days later I call again, and she tells me she has another date.

— Six people say they will help clean up after a neighborhood party at my house. On Saturday morning one shows up.

— I have my new car recalled to replace a defective part.

— I have always believed God is good. I look at a magazine picture story about malnourished kids in the United States. It hits me: how can God be good when people are starving?

— I stay after work for four days in a row to complete an important assignment. My employer accuses me of goofing off on the job.

— I give ten dollars to a charitable

cause and read in the paper that the head of the cause has run off with one hundred thousand dollars.

— A teacher says, "If you study for this test, you'll pass it." I study. I fail. The teacher says, "Why didn't you study?"

— My best friend got stopped by a policeman for speeding. She told him she wasn't speeding, but he wanted her to get in his car. She refused and told him to follow her home, but he drove away. A week later, a story appeared in the paper about a woman getting attacked by a man posing as a policeman.

— A friend gets an A on a paper he copied from a book. I get a C on a paper I worked on for a month.

— I need a new fuel pump for my car. I go to the garage owned by a man who goes to my church. His price seems high, so I go to another garage and discover that the man I know from church is charging almost double.

— I read in the paper about a man who was shot while trying to escape from prison. He spent eleven years behind bars for stealing seventy dollars. He spent eight and a half years in solitary confinement. I ask, how can God let such injustice happen?

Do you find any pattern in the items you considered faithbreakers? Have most of your faithbreaking experiences been caused by friends, by businesses, by religion? Is there a common ideal broken in many cases? Are your ideals realistic?
In what ways are you a faithbreaker?

Study the Sunday newspaper from a major city. In one column list the stories that describe faithbreaking. In a second column list the stories that describe faithkeeping. How do your columns balance out?

"Last night I cried for three hours straight."
"Why?"
"I don't know why."

What has broken your faith in yourself, in others, in God, in your ideals? Talk with a friend about your whys for seemingly unexplainable crying or depression.

To talk about faithbreakers presumes in us a faith to be broken. Following is a list of ten kinds of faith. Number the ten items to show the order in which faith is most likely to be broken.

_____ Personal faith in a name for the unnameable.

_____ Allegiance to the set of beliefs of a church.

_____ Trust in a close friend.

_____ Allegiance to duty or a code of behavior.

_____ Confidence in myself.

_____ Confidence in mass-produced products.

_____ Trust in a parent.

_____ Trust in other drivers.

_____ Faith in a teacher.

_____ Faith in a government official.

Make a personal list of ten people, ideas, codes, or services you believe in. Exchange lists with a friend and indicate where the other's faith may be broken and where it may be kept. Discuss each others' opinions.

With a friend try these person-quake minimizers in three stages.
1. State something you RESENT:
   I resent people who hate each other, who tell me what to do.
2. State your resentment as a DEMAND:
   I demand that people love each other, that they give me a chance.
3. State your resentment and demand as an APPRECIATION:
   I appreciate people who love without expecting return, who try to give me a chance.

Do these statements in any way help you handle your feelings? If so, how? Did you see any broken faith in a new way? If so, how?

Interview three people who serve the public — a doctor, a mechanic, and a grocer; a dentist, a restaurant operator, and a construction worker; a butcher, a factory worker, and a teacher; a bus driver, a telephone operator, and a nurse.... Ask these questions to each of the people you interview:

— What faith would the public have a right to place in you?

— What faith do you have in your customers? Do they take advantage of you?
— What is the most frequent complaint you receive in your dealings with the public?
— Are there any kinds of government specifications you or your business must meet? What are they? Why are they necessary?
— Do people expect more of you than you are trained to do? If so, can you give examples?

Which of the people you interviewed would you confidently advise others to have faith in? What are your reasons? What are the most common reasons for having confidence in someone serving the public? Education? Government standards? Experience? Personality?

Say ten positive things to the same person in the next two days. Choose someone in your family, at school, or on your job. Do not let him or her discover what you are doing. How do the affirming statements affect your relationship with the person?

Do you find that you experience faithbreaking if you expect it, and you experience faithkeeping if you expect it? To what degree do you find either of these expectations true?

Excerpt from a Faith Report

As a young teenager:

I never doubted the existence of God
in those grade school years.
But I don't care what anybody says,
the day you're told there wasn't any
apple
or any special "Adam" is traumatic.
Then the questions pile up,
not screaming in your head
but hammering dully at your vision of
goodness.
During the time I was going through
this,
I can't remember a sunny day.
Maybe it was the season,
but it rained every day.
Buckets, torrents from a world
that had lost its creator.
As God slowly moves out of the part
of you that feels God, loneliness moves in.

It grows the day you ask your mother
if she ever had trouble believing in God
and she says, "no."
When you discover that there are
Christians
who hate, who are prejudiced,
who are indifferent,
Christianity is no longer
good enough for you.

As a young adult:

The hardest part about faith is that it is
bound up with the total person. If it
demanded just
intellectual assent
or dissent,
a "yes" or "no"
would suffice
for a lifetime.
But I, and every other person, have feelings.
My mind says "yes" to God's existence,
but the rest of me revolts against
the idea of an all-powerful person
who knows the Me, the I and Mine.
I wanted concrete proof
for the existence of God,
and I'd be damned if he could
tell me how to live.
I was betrayed by an insider.

I thought I had removed God and
any control he had over me.
I was a completely rational, logical person.
But I hadn't learned that to really reject God,
I would have to reject
my emotions, my mind, my whole self.
I couldn't do that, so I didn't reject God.
Instead, I took in all that "stuff"
I was given in religion —
half the time with the intention
of tearing it apart —
and it grew within me,
until one day a friend loved me,
and then I wanted to break down the walls
so God could come in.
With the birth of friendship,
the sleepless nighttime of faith
ended for me.
A wild and happy reaction followed,
perhaps called "the Lord has come"
syndrome.

Everything became understandable:
the Church, people, God's will,
faith, lack of faith.
It was like being a child again, being
goodness —
only now aware of it.
But faith calms down.
I believed in God, but the world wasn't

immediately changed.
The poor were still with us,
the question of evil was left unanswered,
my family and I still fought,
and peace wasn't.

Every person tends to label certain things
as "holy" or "bad."
I have named a certain part of me the
faithful part.
It's the spirit in me that keeps me
doing things when I can find no reason to:
believe my life will make a difference,
love my friends,
stay awake in class.

What is faith for me now?
It's saying that I'm not sure
exactly what is out there,
but I know it's mine
— I claim it because
a good Man told me I'd want it,
and I know that He is telling the truth.
He died for the truth.

If I hadn't lost my child faith,
I'd never have found out
that I can believe in my own way.
I have discovered the Otherness of God
and some idea of my own uniqueness.

I'll take the doubt — certainty isn't real
without it.

— Kathy Hesse

Write your own faith report.

The problem of evil in the world is a
consistent faithbreaker. Let's ask the
question: "Why have millions of people died
violently in wars in this century?" Can you
select an answer from among the six
statements below and give reasons for your
choice?
— Because of me.
— In evolution there is always waste.
  The balance of life must be
  preserved on the planet.
  Unsuccessful forms become waste
  so new forms can develop.
— The bureaucratic structure piles
  committee upon committee making
  no one responsible for the right or
  wrong of decisions.
— Totalitarian forms of government
  want world power at any expense.
— Because of God.
— Because of the Devil, the
  supernatural enemy of God.

Can you defend any one of these answers without someone poking holes in your argument? Can you arrive at a cause of evil? Why or why not?

Some causes of evil can be determined. Sometimes evil remains mysterious. One couple has a retarded child and demands, "Why did God allow us to have this child?" Another couple has a retarded child and says, "This child with all his needs has brought our family closer together; he has taught us to love."

In *Religion, Language and Truth*, Leslie Dewart, a Catholic theologian, sees the whole human race as free and responsible for history as the individual is free and responsible for his or her life.

He believes that, given the reality of human freedom, humanity's creation of history could take place without, and even against, God. "The real ability of men and women — given enough time — to create any possible world, means that, if we want to we can create the sort of world in which there is no room for God, and the sort of history which dispenses with moral requirements transcending man himself.

The creation of such a world is what Christianity has traditionally called *sin*, and the outcome of such history is what Christianity has traditionally called *hell*."

What do you think of Dewart's idea that the human race is free to create a hell on earth? Do you think that believing that God would somehow bring good out of evil has prevented us from seeing how responsible we are for our world? What kind of world would you like to see earth evolve into? How could you help it happen?

Chapter Five

Making a Revelation

Make light of the darkness.
Warm the cold.
Gather in twos and threes and more
and find
WHO and WHAT
IS in your midst.

A true speaking word reveals meaning.
It opens up the significance of an event. It
communicates something of the inside self.
In conversation, we reveal ourselves —
something of ourselves is opened to the
view of others.

We are often mysteriously touched by
the revelation of a person's inside or by the
breakthrough of the meaning of an event.
We can't quite understand how it happened.
We sense something extra — a gift
dimension to the conversation. Each person
tries to express himself or herself. More
understanding is opened up together than
each person individually contributes.

Words for what is happening in a
conversation, like sparks, ignite a chain of

knowing among us. Together, we share a revelation. The significance, the meaning of a conversation is something we create as we express and name what is happening in a group. We reveal ourselves when each of us has the courage to speak from his or her inside.

Twenty people gathered one Sunday night to share their thoughts about faith and growth. Some of the twenty had been gathering together every other Sunday night for three years as a church study group. Some joined the group for the first time that night. Dick and Dolores were the moderators. They were all Christians. The words they shared with each other revealed their faith.

As you read their conversation you will probably realize that some found words for their beliefs for the first time. The readings and discussion of the evening were taped and condensed. Hopefully, they will help you and groups you know share together, help each other find God in your midst.

About Seeds and Bread

Marie: The theme of our celebration is growth and faith.

Casey: (Reads over background music.) "One day a farmer went out sowing. Part of what he sowed landed on a footpath, where birds came and ate it up. Part of it fell on rocky ground, where it had little soil. It sprouted at once since the soil had no depth, but when the sun rose and scorched it, it began to wither for lack of roots. Again, part of the seed fell among thorns, which grew up and choked it. Part of it, finally, landed on good soil and yielded grain a hundred – or sixty – or thirtyfold." (Matthew 13:4-9 NAB)
    The seed is the word of God spoken to us. The seed takes faith and love to grow. Many listen but do not respond to the word. This is not growing. Praise the Lord, thank him, believe in him, love him, and listen to him. Remember also that this is only half of your growth. Praise your fellow human beings, thank them, believe in them, love them and listen to them. This makes growth complete.

Great will be the reward to those who
praise, thank, believe, love, and listen. On
earth as in heaven, you will receive a
hundredfold from God and all people.
The word of God is the seed of growth.
Faith and love — the sunshine and rain.

Lynn: Jesus confused people who came to
hear him. He claimed that doing the work of
God was believing in him. The people
wanted a sign to show that he was from
God. Bread, Jesus said, was his sign.

I myself am the bread of life.
No one who comes to me shall ever be
     hungry,
No one who believes in me shall ever thirst.
...If anyone eats this bread
he shall live forever;
the bread I will give
is my flesh, for the life of the world.
(John 6:35, 51 NAB)

Brenda: (Begins a discussion of the
readings.) Bread is really something that
everyone can associate with. Meat is not so
basic, but bread is always there.

Jon: But bread is made; it's not just there.
Someone puts the bread together and bakes

it. It's not there until you make it. Jesus saying he is the bread of life is like saying that he has to be put together by us in order to mean something in our lives.

Tim: I like the idea that bread is something made. As long as wheat is in the ground, it can continue growing. But as soon as the grain becomes flour and bread, it can only grow if it becomes part of the human body. It's useable only if somebody makes it a part of himself or herself.

Dolores: You mean God is saying to me, "You're what I need."? Isn't it what he does with me that's going to make me a great thing?

Dick: I have trouble understanding Jesus' statement, "I am the bread of life, and he who eats this bread will live forever." I think there's a real literal sense to what he's saying. I really want to believe it; I keep hoping that I will.

Julie: I don't believe it really — I've just always accepted Communion without really thinking or feeling that it was true. I don't laugh at it, but there's been real doubt in my mind. I've thought a lot about how great a person Christ was to take on the sins of the world. But faith is the hardest thing for me.

Love is something you can see and respond to. It takes more strength to have faith. I don't want to accept things blindly. I want to know why I believe in God.

Joe: That's the way I am too. I have to be logical about it.

Diane: I really believe that God is good and just. I think that is faith.

Michelle: My faith is really simple. I try to plan so that everything I do has some purpose that will add good to somebody else's life or make a difference in the world. But it's hard to accept things as they are and work slowly. I get discouraged.

Joe: Any energy that is capable of creating a universe such as this, with all the galaxies and solar systems, is really something. There are people who think the universe is expanding. And they also think that chances of life on earth were sort of one in a million. The earth is such a small place in the universe, but I think that anyone who would have the power to create this — I call that person God — also has the power to care about all the people. That's what makes me pull out of a conversation sometimes and say "Thanks God." I guess that's what I call faith.

Jon: Like you said, Joe, the universe is so tremendously immense, and we don't have any comprehension at all about how big it could possibly be. And yet, here we are and we're so important to ourselves.

Diane: Exactly, there's got to be something behind us to make such little things as we are so important.

Joe: Like those fantastic pictures of the brain you see in magazines. All those different channels and switches. It makes you know that we didn't evolve just by accident. We can consider ourselves tiny. But then consider what else is tiny compared to us. It's just as amazing how little things are as how immense.

Dick: I think in all of the conversation tonight, there is one basic underlying truth behind everybody's statements. There's a feeling that somewhere down underneath all of this there is a truth and unity that makes us all one. Identify it as God, Jesus, there's a basic truth. Now let's take this bread and pass it among us. And in our own way let's share it and its meaning for us with each other.

Each person pulled a chunk of bread from the loaf. Someone suggested exchanging little pieces of each other's bread to show unity. Everybody shared bread with the person next to him or her. Then Joe, Brenda, and Jon got up and moved around, and ten minutes later every person there had exchanged bread and a bit of themselves with every other person.

Everyone felt a special happening in the group that night. Faith seemed no longer just a word. It had come alive. As person after person spoke from the inside, it freed others. Something more happened in the group than anyone alone could make happen. The openness in each person created a "yes" feeling in the group.

Plan your own celebration of your faith and growth alone, with a friend or with a group.

Chapter Six

Waking

I am and what will I become?
Others are and what will they become?
The universe is and what energy,
what silence surrounds us unnamed?
Picture yourself, a person,
a maker of meaning on the beach.
You stand at the shore;
before you lies the sea of all possibilities.
You stand on sand wet and receptive
to waves of the unknown.
What do you make of yourself,
you with your feet washed
by the world's spin and the moon's pull?
Will you build intricate castles with walls
and moats?
Will you play with the shells and weeds
washed ashore?
Will you write in the sand?
Walk with welcoming arms into the waves?
In the silence between the breakers,
what do you hear?

Faith in God is not childish fantasy.
It is the purposeful search
of the mature person,
answering for the fact
he or she is alive and awake.
Each of us is a unique openness
to life around us.
Each of us is a unique expression
of life as it happens to us.
Each of us is rooted
in the mysterious fact: we live.

The American poet Theodore Roethke
calls a life lived in search of meaning, "The
Waking."

For us, the people on the beach,
standing on the shore of the known,
facing the unknown,
he writes:

I wake to sleep and take my waking slow,
...I learn by going where I have to go.